Deleted.

Books should be returned or renewed by the last date
above. Renew by phone **08458 247 200** or online
*www.kent.gov.uk/libs*

**Libraries & Archives**

CUSTOMER
SERVICE
EXCELLENCE

UK

The Government Standard

# REAL LIVES

# Winston Churchill

*Harriet Castor*

A & C BLACK • LONDON

*In memory of my grandfather,*
*Leslie Watson, who served in North Africa and my*
*great-uncle, John Davies, who served in the Middle East*
*during World War II.*

First published 2012 by
A & C Black, an imprint of Bloomsbury Publishing Plc
50 Bedford Square, London, WC1B 3DP

www.acblack.com
www.bloomsbury.com

ISBN 978-1-4081-3117-6

A CIP catalogue for this book is available from the British Library.

Printed and bound in Great Britain
by CPI Cox & Wyman, Reading RG1 8EX

1 3 5 7 9 10 8 6 4 2

# Contents

# 1
# War in Africa

*Boom! Bang!* The explosions were terrifying. Enemy soldiers, hidden in the hills beside the railway track, were firing on the train with rifles and big field guns.

"It's an ambush!" yelled Captain Haldane from his wagon. "Driver – go faster!"

The train – full of British soldiers in open-topped armoured trucks – raced ahead. It was crossing Natal, a British-held area in South Africa. The year was 1899 and a bloody war was raging between the British and the Boers – Dutch-speaking settlers who had lived in South Africa for several generations.

The railway track led downhill. Helped by the slope, the train was now going very fast. In one of the rear trucks, a newspaper war reporter stood among the soldiers. He turned to Captain Haldane. "We're going too fast, aren't we? It's unsafe. Should I climb along to the engine and tell the driver to slow down?"

Before Haldane could reply, there was an enormous bang and jolt from the front of the train. Everyone in the truck was thrown to the floor.

The newspaper reporter was the first to scramble to his feet. Quickly he climbed up to look over the side of the truck. The train was now at the bottom of the hill. On the grassy slopes above, he could see enemy soldiers running closer. The next moment heavy rifle-fire began whistling through the air and clanging against the steel-plated sides of the train.

"We're sitting ducks!" exclaimed the reporter, jumping back down. He turned to the army captain. "I'm at your service, Haldane."

Captain Haldane knew this man: though he was a war reporter, he'd been trained as a soldier. He and Haldane had been stationed together in India and Haldane trusted him completely.

"Find out what's happened to the front of the train," said Haldane. "See if you can clear the line. I'll organise the men at the back here to return fire."

The reporter obeyed immediately. He pushed his way out of the truck and ran down the length of the train. Bullets screeched overhead. He found the engine still on the line. But in front of it, two trucks had been derailed and were lying across the track. Ahead of them, another truck had flipped over completely. Some of the men who'd been riding on it were obviously dead; others were badly injured.

The reporter checked the track. The reason for the crash was clear: the Boers had put a rock on the line.

"I'm getting out of here!"

The reporter whipped round to see who had spoken.

"I'm a civilian! What am I paid for? To be blown to bits?" It was the driver, staggering from the engine, his face streaming with blood where a piece of shrapnel had hit him.

*If we lose him we're doomed*, thought the reporter. *He's the only man who knows how to drive the train.*

As the driver stumbled past, the reporter caught him by the elbow. "Think – no one's ever hit twice on the same day, are they?" he said. "Do your duty now and you'll get a medal for gallantry – you may never get the chance of one again!"

The driver stared. Who was this man? Not an army commander – he was dressed like a civilian. Yet here he was, taking charge. He looked young – only in his twenties. But, as the shells detonated around them, all the driver could see in his bright blue eyes was rock-steady determination and something almost like delight.

Suddenly the driver felt more confident. He wiped the blood from his face with his sleeve and headed back for the engine cab.

"Good man!" the reporter called after him. "I'll stick with you!"

Under a hail of fire, the reporter ran towards some soldiers sheltering behind their wrecked truck. "I need twenty volunteers," he said calmly, "to help me get these trucks out of the way of the engine."

For the next hour the reporter took charge, directing the operation as the soldiers tried to push the immensely heavy wrecked trucks off the track, helped by the engine shunting to and fro. There were hold-ups and problems. Many soldiers were wounded and some were killed.

At last, the engine managed to push past the trucks that were blocking the line. The reporter ran to ask Captain Haldane for permission to evacuate the wounded. Then he and the driver hauled more than twenty bleeding men onto the engine and tender. When they had finished the space was so crammed that there was barely room for the two of them to climb onto the footplate.

Then the engine started off, heading for the safety of the nearest British-held station. But after half a mile, the reporter jumped down and began walking back the way they had come.

"Where are you going?" yelled the driver.

"Back to help the others!" the reporter replied.

"He's worth fifty soldiers, that one," muttered the driver, shaking his head in amazement. "Do you know his name?" he asked the nearest wounded man.

The soldier managed a grin. "Churchill. Winston Churchill." Then he spotted something lying on a ledge above the firebox. "God help him – look. He's left his pistol behind."

# 2
# Prisoner of War

"Another letter from that British man Churchill, sir." A Boer soldier handed the paper to his commanding officer, General Joubert. "Says that since he's only a newspaper reporter, he shouldn't be held as a prisoner of war."

After stepping off the engine, Churchill had gone back along the railway track only to be confronted by Boer fighters aiming their rifles at him. He reached for his pistol, but found he was completely unarmed. There was no choice but to surrender. Marched back to the place of the derailment by his captors, he saw that Captain Haldane and his troops had been taken prisoner too. Now they were all imprisoned in camps in a Boer-controlled area of South Africa called the Transvaal.

General Joubert scanned the letter and shook his

head. "Only a newspaper reporter? I don't believe anything of the kind. He's dangerous. And the British newspapers are making him out to be a hero. No, he must not be released until the end of the war – whenever that comes."

And so, in November 1899, Churchill spent his 25th birthday as a prisoner. He could not bear being cooped up; he could not bear that the exciting events of the war were going on without him. Above all, he could not bear the thought that time was ticking away. His father, Lord Randolph Churchill, had died at the age of forty-five. Winston was convinced that he would die young too. His burning desire was to be famous and to achieve great things, but he feared there was not much time left.

Daring and desperately impatient, Churchill soon escaped from the prisoner-of-war camp. The escape had been planned with Captain Haldane and another British officer but, in the event, only Churchill managed to get over the wall.

Without his friends, Churchill's situation looked hopeless. He was deep in enemy territory with no compass – Haldane was to have brought that – and no map. All he had were the clothes he stood up in,

£75, and four slabs of chocolate. Before him lay a three-hundred-mile walk to safety.

During the next nine days, Churchill experienced hunger, exhaustion and, at his lowest moments, despair. The Boers were scouring the countryside for him. They had put up 'Wanted' posters, offering a reward to anyone who handed him in, dead or alive. But at last – aided by some British miners who helped him hide down their mine and then in the wagon of a goods train – Churchill made it out of Boer-held territory. He could have boarded a boat for Britain and safety, but instead he decided to go straight back to the front line.

It was Christmas Eve when Churchill reached the British commander's Natal headquarters. The HQ was in the exact spot where Churchill's train had been derailed and ambushed just over a month before.

The commander, General Buller, greeted Churchill warmly and asked him many questions about the enemy territory he had travelled through.

"You have done very well," Buller said at last. "Is there anything we can do for you?"

Churchill smiled eagerly. "I should like to rejoin the army, sir, please," he said.

# 3
# Young Churchill

As a child, Winston Churchill had owned over a thousand toy soldiers, and had spent many hours arranging them in battle formations in the nursery at his parents' grand house. These were the happy times, in the school holidays; by contrast Churchill's schooldays had been utterly miserable. He was sent to a series of boarding schools, one of which believed in flogging disobedient pupils until they bled. Many of Churchill's teachers considered him wilful, naughty and careless, but to his fellow-pupils he seemed brave and charismatic – an independent character who was ready to say what he thought.

Churchill had two ambitions: to be a soldier and a politician. In those days, politicians were as famous as TV stars today. Even though the only people allowed to vote were men who owned a house, paid a certain amount of rent or had a certain amount of money, almost everyone, rich and poor, followed the latest reports from Parliament with as much interest as they now follow football matches or talent shows.

Churchill's own father, Lord Randolph, was a politician. He was a cold, strict parent but Winston adored him and wanted to follow in his footsteps. Lord Randolph had other ideas: his ambition was for Winston to become a barrister. However, as bad report after bad report followed Winston home from school, Lord Randolph decided his son was not clever enough for the law. He would have to join the army instead.

So, at the age of eighteen, Churchill joined the Royal Military Academy at Sandhurst, where he trained as a cavalry officer. He loved studying the tactics and strategy of warfare, and did very well.

He had wanted to spend a few years as a soldier and then become a Member of Parliament alongside his father. But Lord Randolph died soon after Churchill left Sandhurst. Churchill's dream of at last getting to know his father was shattered, and now he had money worries, too: his parents had lived lavishly, but without the necessary income. He had to find a way to help support his mother and his younger brother, as well as himself.

Churchill's American mother, Lady Jennie, was famed for her beauty and charm, and had many high-level connections in London's upper class society. Encouraging Jennie to pull all the strings she could, Churchill tried to get himself sent to every active theatre of war in the British Empire. When possible, he went as a soldier. When that was impossible, he went as a newspaper war reporter. In either case, he wrote reports on what he saw and sold them to the papers back home.

His reports were exciting and well written; soon Churchill was the highest paid war reporter in Britain. He followed up his articles with best-selling books about his travels. He became famous and, though several military commanders thought him too much of an attention-seeker, he gained a reputation for immense personal courage.

In the summer of 1900, Churchill returned to Britain after his astonishing experiences in the Boer War – as reporter, prisoner of war and soldier. He was 25 and he believed his life would be short, so there was no time to lose: now it was time to hang up his spurs and turn to the second of his ambitions – politics.

# 4
# Conservative to Liberal

"Winston Leonard Spencer Churchill," the election official read out from his list. "12,931 votes."

"Yes!" yelled the Conservative Party supporters in the hall.

The man standing beside Churchill on the platform grasped his hand and shook it warmly. "By Jove, Winston, you've done it!"

Churchill beamed with delight, and allowed himself to be swept along to the local Conservative Party offices on a tide of supporters, all waving flags and cheering themselves hoarse.

It was October 1st 1900. Less than three months after returning from South Africa, Churchill had been elected the Member of Parliament (or MP) for Oldham in Greater Manchester.

At that time in Britain there were two main

political parties: the Conservatives and the Liberals. Churchill – just like his father before him – was a Conservative. But (also just like his father before him) he was always prepared to say what he thought was right, even if it went against Conservative Party policy.

Now, as a new MP, Churchill voted in Parliament against the use of Chinese slave labour in British-controlled parts of South Africa. He voted in support of legal rights for Trades Unions. He voted against an anti-asylum bill that would, he feared, limit the number of refugees who could flee to Britain to escape persecution abroad. Each time, he was voting against the Conservative Party. Many of his neighbours on the Conservative benches in the House of Commons became very annoyed.

When Churchill began to make speeches in the Commons in support of free trade, it was the last straw. Free trade meant allowing open competition, without the government adding fees to the prices of foreign goods to make them less attractive for buyers. Churchill thought that free trade was the best way to keep prices low, and therefore help the poor. But some Conservatives wanted goods from

Britain and the British Empire to be protected.

On March 29th 1904, when Churchill stood up to make a speech in support of free trade, most of the Conservative MPs around him walked out of the Commons.

"It was awfully disconcerting," said Churchill afterwards as he stood in the Commons bar with a Welsh Liberal MP named David Lloyd George.

"It was rude, you mean," said Lloyd George, sipping a soda water. "Shockingly rude!"

Churchill scowled into his brandy. "Do you know, I'd rather they'd interrupted me – at least then I could have answered them. Even laughing at me would have been better. To feel them melting away behind me was..." He hesitated, then took a large sip of his drink. "Well, I must say it was an effort to finish the speech."

"You'll be a Liberal before long," said Lloyd George. "That's my view. You're voting with us often enough. Face facts, Winston – you've a Liberal heart!"

Churchill pushed out his lower lip, considering. "I've an independent heart, I think," he said.

Nevertheless, Lloyd George was right: on May 31st 1904 Churchill did cross the floor of the

House of Commons and join the Liberal Party. Straight away, he became one of the most energetic critics of Conservative policy.

As a result, he earned many enemies. And they were enemies who would dog him for a long time to come.

However, for the moment Churchill's career was going well. In 1906 the Liberals won a general election and within two years Churchill had become a cabinet minister, as President of the Board of Trade. At 33, he was very young for the job. Lloyd George had risen to high office too: he was Chancellor of the Exchequer. Together they worked to bring in new laws that would help the poor.

Churchill had been deeply shocked to read a study of poverty in York that showed a quarter of workers were not paid enough to feed their families. He felt so passionate about fighting poverty that his new fiancée, Miss Clementine Hozier, was worried he would have no time for her once they were married.

Churchill, enthusiastic and energetic as ever, persuaded Clementine that he would make time for everything and in September 1908 they were married at St Margaret's Church, Westminster – the parish church of the House of Commons.

Clementine had been right about Churchill's commitment to his work, though: in the vestry after the service, he was so busy talking about politics that he almost forgot to escort his bride out of the church.

# 5

# The Great War

In June 1914, a murder took place that was to change the course of world history. The Emperor of Austria-Hungary's heir – his nephew – was shot dead along with his wife in Sarajevo, a city that was then part of the Austro-Hungarian Empire. The assassin was a young man from the neighbouring Kingdom of Serbia.

The Emperor, Franz Joseph, hadn't liked his nephew. To him, the shooting wasn't a tragedy – it was an opportunity. He wanted to declare war on Serbia. And now his nephew's assassination gave him the perfect excuse.

Franz Joseph wanted war with Serbia because the people who lived there were mostly Slavs. He believed that a bloody struggle for dominance of Europe was coming – and that the struggle would be between the Germanic peoples (who included Austrians and Germans) and the Slav peoples (who included Serbs and Russians). Franz Joseph was afraid of Russia and afraid, too, of the Slavs living in or close to his own territories, especially those in Serbia. In fact, he believed that Serbia was so dangerous it must be destroyed.

But Franz Joseph knew that if he declared war on Serbia, Russia might come to Serbia's aid. And if that happened, he would need an ally of his own: Germany. So, before acting against Serbia, Franz Joseph asked the German government whether it would support him if a war began.

The answer was a definite yes. More than that: a delighted yes. The German Army commanders were well prepared for war, and they knew that the Russians were not. Just like Franz Joseph, they believed that war between Russia and Germany was inevitable. So they were keen that it should happen now, before Russia could get ready.

In London, Churchill was following these developments with sharp interest. He had known for a long time that Germany was preparing for war. His colleagues in the Liberal Government thought he was over-anxious when he insisted that the British Navy should get ready too. Now he was about to be proved right.

Churchill was still a cabinet minister, but his job had changed. After being President of the Board of Trade he had spent a year and a half as Home Secretary. Then, in 1911, he had become First Lord of the Admiralty, which meant he was in charge of the navy. For the whole of the three years since then, he had worked desperately hard at preparing the British fleet for war.

Knowing that Germany would be trying to invent new weapons, Churchill took a keen interest in new technology. He supported the development of submarines. He took lessons in how torpedoes worked. And he became fascinated by one of the newest branches of 'war science': the use of aeroplanes.

Churchill was convinced that aeroplanes were vitally important: while the Army saw them as observation and information-gathering devices, Churchill believed that, one day, battles would take place in the air.

At the beginning of August 1914, just over a month after the shooting in Sarajevo, Germany declared war on Russia, on France (Russia's ally) and on Belgium too. The Liberal Government believed Britain must help France and Belgium. So at 7 p.m. on August 4th an ultimatum was delivered to Germany: if she did not promise by midnight German time (11 p.m. London time) to withdraw, Britain would declare war.

Churchill spent that evening at the Admiralty, in the War Room. It was filled with staff, but everyone was quiet and tense: Churchill could hear the clock ticking.

The windows were wide open. The warm air of the summer evening drifted in, along with sounds from the crowds who had gathered in the streets outside, waiting for news. As 11 o'clock approached, from the direction of Buckingham Palace the distant singing of hundreds of voices could be heard: "God Save the King". And then – deep and booming – Big Ben began to chime the hour.

The War Room staff knew what to do. The telegram giving the signal to all the ships of the British navy that war had started was sent immediately. Churchill left the room.

He walked across Horse Guards Parade to No. 10 Downing Street. There, in the Cabinet Room, with the curtains undrawn so that the black night sky was clearly visible in all its vastness beyond, sat the Prime Minister and his Cabinet colleagues. They all looked up as Churchill entered – and the expression on every face was grave.

"Prime Minister, gentlemen." Churchill nodded to them in solemn greeting. "It is done. The telegram has been sent. We are at war with Germany."

# 6

# Inventing the Tank

Some people in Britain were so confident of a swift victory that they thought the war would be over by Christmas. But by Christmas 1914, instead of victory there was deadlock.

The German army had advanced into Belgium and France. The British and French armies had managed to stop the Germans, but not to push them into retreat. Both sides came to a halt. Both dug defensive channels in the earth called trenches from which to shoot at one another, and protected the trenches with barbed wire. By Christmas 1914 the trenches stretched in an unbroken line for more than 350 miles, from the Swiss Alps in the south to the Belgian coast in the north, where the barbed wire curled right down the beach into the waves.

Two months later, in February 1915, there was a

secret meeting at the Admiralty. Churchill was ill with 'flu, so the meeting took place in his bedroom. It was hardly surprising that he was unwell – since long before the outbreak of war he had worked feverishly, sleeping little, involving himself not only in every aspect of navy action, but taking a deep interest in the land war too. He had been to France several times, and seen the trenches for himself.

"Nothing like this has ever been known in the whole history of warfare!" he declared now, sitting propped up in bed in his dressing gown, his face pale. "With such a long continuous front line there is absolutely no possibility of manoeuvre!"

Three men sat listening: Mr d'Eyncourt, the Chief Constructor of the navy; Major Hetherington, an officer from an armoured-car squadron; and Colonel Dumble of the Naval Brigade, a former Royal Engineer.

"And with firepower what it is these days, it is suicide to attack the front head-on," said Major Hetherington. "We all know the slaughter that is taking place in France now. What was that figure you mentioned to me yesterday, sir? 300,000 Frenchmen dead in the last five months?"

Churchill nodded grimly. "The lives and the

magnificent courage of these soldiers are being squandered," he said. "The problem is mechanical: gunfire. Therefore the solution must be mechanical too. It is no use putting body after body in the way of the bullets and expecting a breakthrough. Some contraption must be invented so that soldiers can advance towards the enemy protected by steel plating. Major Hetherington – please describe the 'land battleship' idea for these gentlemen."

"With pleasure." Hetherington turned to d'Eyncourt and Dumble. "Picture this: a steam tractor carrying on its back a bullet-proof shelter large enough to contain men and machine-guns. The wheels would be fitted with caterpillar tracks, so that the vehicle could cross trenches. It would be able to crush lines of barbed wire, too."

Mr d'Eyncourt leaned forward. "We'll need an expert in heavy traction."

"I know just the man," said Colonel Dumble. "A Royal Engineer, serves under Colonel Crompton – "

Listening to the discussion, Churchill felt delighted and energised, despite his illness. He was taking a risk – he had not informed the War Office about this meeting. He had already discovered that the military authorities had no faith either that landships *could* be made, or that they would be any use if they were. Churchill had been told to stop meddling and stick to navy matters. Now, in giving orders for experiments and providing funds for them, Churchill was acting outside his proper powers. But he knew that if he didn't do it, no one else would.

"There is no time to lose," d'Eyncourt was saying. "We must bear in mind that the Germans will be working on their own inventions too – who knows when they will launch some entirely new weapon at our troops?"

"The Germans must not get wind of what we are developing," added Dumble. "The designs for these landships must carry false labels in case they fall into the wrong hands. What could we call them?"

There was a short silence.

"'Water-carriers for Russia'?" suggested d'Eyncourt.

"That might get shortened to 'WCs for Russia'," said Dumble. Everyone laughed.

"How about 'Water-Tanks for Russia'?" said Churchill.

Eventually the landships came to be called simply 'tanks' for short. And the name stuck.

# 7
# Forced Out

Late into the night, across the dark expanse of Horse Guards Parade, the lights in Churchill's rooms at the Admiralty could be seen shining. There, Churchill and his assistants sat up night after night, trying to find ways to bring the war to a swift end.

With the Western Front in deadlock, Churchill looked for other places where a telling blow could be landed on the German forces or their allies. One possible place was Turkey.

Turkey was fighting as an ally of Germany. An attack on Turkey would have several advantages. It would draw German troops and ships away from Western Europe, to join in Turkey's defence. It would help Russia, Britain's ally, which was suffering Turkish attacks. And, it was hoped, it would encourage Greece, Bulgaria and Romania to join the war on the British side.

The suggested place for an attack was the Dardanelles, a narrow strait (channel of water) in northwest Turkey. An attack on the Dardanelles was not only Churchill's idea – others suggested it too. The War Council liked the plan, and preparations began.

Churchill's role at the Admiralty involved working very closely with the First Sea Lord, who was the most senior admiral in charge of running the Royal Navy. Churchill had appointed Lord Fisher, a 73 year-old retired admiral, to the job.

During preparations for the Dardanelles campaign Lord Fisher kept changing his mind. One day he would argue for a navy-only attack, the next he would threaten to resign unless the army were involved too. What's more, the head of the army, Lord Kitchener, could not decide either. He changed his mind three times about whether troops would be available for the Dardanelles.

The result was a mess, and the campaign began to go very badly.

On May 15th 1915, Lord Fisher suddenly resigned, giving no reason except that he could not work with Churchill any more.

For the Prime Minister, Herbert Asquith, this was a crisis. His Liberal Government was already being criticised by the Conservatives for the way it was handling the war. Now, with Lord Fisher's resignation, the Government seemed to be in a shambles. The Conservatives threatened to vote the government down unless Asquith agreed to form a coalition: a government of Liberals and Conservatives working together.

The following Monday, Churchill went to see Asquith in his rooms at the House of Commons. Asquith told him about the new demand.

Churchill nodded. "I am very much in favour of a coalition government," he said. "But could you delay its formation until I have appointed the new First Sea Lord and things are settled at the Admiralty?"

Asquith sighed, and tapped the papers on the desk in front of him. "I am afraid, Winston, that will not be possible. The Conservatives refuse to work with us unless you leave the Admiralty."

Churchill snorted. "There's no need to give in to that kind of bullying! I have prepared a speech to deliver in the Commons, defending every decision taken over the Dardanelles. I expect a fierce debate with the Conservatives, but I am equal to it."

Churchill knew many Conservatives still hated him because he had switched parties. He knew, too, that they blamed him for everything that had gone wrong so far with the Dardanelles campaign. He was determined to press on despite them, and make it a success.

Sorrowfully Asquith shook his head. "I'm sorry, Winston, but there's nothing I can do."

Churchill stared at the Prime Minister, aghast. He had spent three years preparing for war – he had seen it coming long before anyone else. His enemies could not now snatch all power to help with the war effort away from him – could they?

# 8

# Country Exile

In the bright summer sunlight, the Surrey countryside looked lush and green. A breeze gently stirred the long grass in the fields around the farm, and birds called to one another from the treetops.

In the farmhouse garden, Churchill sat on a bench, his head in his hands.

"Papa?" said a small voice.

Churchill looked up. It was his oldest child, six-year-old Diana. She climbed onto the bench beside him. "Poor Papa," she said, stroking his shoulder. "I love staying here for our holidays. I wish you loved it too. Why are you so gloomy?"

Churchill struggled to smile at his daughter. Most of the time, these days, he felt he was lost in an ocean of despair. "I am not gloomy about staying here," he said. "I am gloomy about the war.

It is not going terribly well, you see. I know how to fix it, and I tell people what needs to be done – over and over – but no one will listen to me any more."

His old Conservative enemies had won: Churchill had had to leave the Admiralty. He was 40 years old and his career looked like it was finished. Meanwhile the Dardanelles campaign was continuing, but Churchill was not allowed to be involved. The army attack was going badly and thousands of soldiers were dying.

Diana looked solemn. "But why does no one listen to you, Papa? You are a very important person!"

A rash person, the Conservatives said – and the newspapers, too. A dangerous, irresponsible person. The blame for the Dardanelles disaster was being put entirely on Churchill, even though Kitchener and Fisher had contributed so much to the problems.

It ate away at Churchill that he could not clear his name. He wanted to explain everything that had happened. Even more than that, he wanted to be involved in the war planning now, so that he could help the poor soldiers who were out there this very minute, fighting and dying.

He looked at his daughter. "Do you think I am a very important person, Diana?"

"Yes. I *know* so."

"Well, I have always thought so too. But – and I know this will shock you deeply –" He lifted the blonde hair that hung over her ear and whispered, "...not everyone agrees with us."

"Come on, Daddy." Diana squirmed off the bench and tugged at his hand. "Aunt Goonie's doing a painting. I want you to see."

Churchill's brother Jack was in the army, serving in the Dardanelles. Churchill was desperately worried about him, as was Jack's wife Gwendoline, or 'Goonie'. Now, led by Diana, Churchill found his sister-in-law in another part of the garden, absorbed in painting a picture.

"Try it," she said, holding out a brush to Churchill. "I find it helps. Look – there's a spare canvas."

Churchill had never painted before. Now, as he attacked the canvas with energy and total concentration, he found that the activity calmed and soothed him.

That summer, Churchill spent many hours

painting pictures. And as he painted, he realised what he wanted to do – what he must do. He would go to the Western Front – the trenches – and join the fight.

# 9

# Return to War

"Gentlemen," said Churchill, looking round at his officers, "this regiment is responsible for a thousand yards of the front line. I demand keen vigilance from each and every man at all times. But I also demand this: good humour. Laugh when you get the chance and encourage your men to do the same. And if you can't smile, keep out of the way until you can."

When Churchill had said he wanted to join the Army in France, friends had offered him safe jobs – but he had turned them down. Instead he took command of a battalion of Royal Scots Fusiliers who were stationed at the Belgian village of Ploegsteert – or, as the British soldiers called it, 'Plug Street'.

Conditions in the trenches were horrifying, and thousands of men were dying. Churchill threw himself into organising and encouraging his battalion.

Making his way now over the uneven muddy ground, past shell craters and blasted trees, Churchill climbed down into the nearest trench. He inspected its walls. "These parapets must be thick enough to stop a bullet," he said, patting the top edge of the wall. "MacDavid, organise a team of men to work on it."

"Yes, sir."

"How are the men in this section?" he asked a private, who was standing to attention near one of the shelters, or 'dugouts'.

"Everyone's still talking about the sports day and concert you organised for us, sir," said the soldier. "It really lifted the spirits of the men."

"You won one of the events, didn't you?" said Churchill. "Pillow-fight, wasn't it?"

The soldier grinned. "That's right, sir."

"A noble victory. Well, I think your skills will be well suited to getting this dugout properly sandbagged. A sandbag's just a harder sort of pillow, after all."

The men under Churchill's command had been suspicious of him at first – but soon they came to love him. They were astonished by how hard he worked, by his fearlessness under fire and by his cheerfulness despite the dreadful conditions. They also thought him eccentric: he had brought his easel from England, and spent spare moments painting pictures of his shell-battered HQ.

Though totally committed to his men, Churchill never took his eye off the London political scene. What he wanted above all was another job in government. The question was: when and how could he get one?

After five and half months, Churchill's battalion was merged with another, under a different commander. Churchill came back to Britain. He hoped he would be offered a government job straight away, but it didn't happen. For a year he waited, frustrated and depressed. He disagreed intensely with the strategy the military commanders were following. Huge numbers of troops were being killed, but he could do nothing about it.

At last, in the summer of 1917, Churchill was made Minister of Munitions. This meant he was in charge of the manufacture and supply of weapons and war equipment. It was not a senior government post – it didn't mean he could return to the War Council. But it was right at the heart of the war effort, and that was where Churchill wanted above all to be. He was delighted.

The Conservatives, by contrast, were appalled. A hundred Conservative MPs signed a request for a debate in Parliament, in protest at his appointment.

By now, Churchill's friend Lloyd George had taken over from Asquith as Prime Minister. Lloyd George knew Churchill's fantastic talents. But above all, he valued Churchill's ability to raise everyone's spirits – including his own.

Lloyd George was not disappointed. Churchill plunged into his job as Minister of Munitions with whirlwind energy. He worked incredibly long hours and took to sleeping at his office. Even the Conservatives were, grudgingly, impressed.

At last, in November 1918, Germany surrendered and the 'Great War' was over. For the past four years Churchill had worked tirelessly and had achieved a great deal, but in the public mind he was still connected above all to one disaster.

After the war, when Churchill spoke at public meetings, he began regularly to be interrupted by hecklers. And they always shouted the same thing: "What about the Dardanelles?"

# 10
# Liberal to Conservative

Within four years of the end of the war, Churchill lost his seat at a general election. Not only was he no longer a government minister, he was now no longer even an MP. For the second time, his political career seemed to be over.

Churchill was heartbroken, but he had to keep working. He employed many staff and loved luxuries such as champagne, so he was always in need of money. His best route to earning it was writing.

Tormented by the popular belief that the disasters of the Dardanelles campaign had been entirely his fault, Churchill began to write his own vast account of the Great War (now called the First World War). During this time, he bought a large house in Kent called Chartwell and here, in his spacious study, he strode up and down, dictating to a fast-typing secretary.

"The year 1915 – the year of the Dardanelles campaign – was the turning point of the Great War," he declared, while in the corner of the room the secretary's fingers flitted over the typewriter keys. "It was disastrous for the Allies, and disastrous for the world. The events of 1915 ensured that the cost of eventual victory for the Allies was so high, that it seemed hardly different from defeat..."

Churchill stopped at one of the windows. He and Clementine had four children now – three girls and a boy – and he could see them playing outside in the garden. A fourth girl had died, aged only two, a few years before, and not a day went past when Churchill did not think of her.

"Start a new section," he said, still watching his children. "The quarrels and hatreds festering between the peoples of Europe have not been settled by the Great War. They continue to this day. The Allied victory – bought at such a terrible cost – has failed to remove the dangers that began the war. Is this the end? Or is it just another chapter in a terrible, blood-soaked story? Are the three great powers – France,

Germany and Russia – doomed to renew their fight? Will our children shed their blood on the devastated lands of Europe?"

Churchill believed not only that the First World War had failed to settle the problems of Europe but that those problems were getting much, much worse.

He was especially worried about communism. Before the end of the war, there had been a revolution in Russia and the ruling royal family had been killed. The Russian Empire had become a communist state called the Soviet Union. Churchill believed that communism was the worst tyranny in history. He feared that Germany might become a communist state too. He was even worried about Britain.

Churchill's hatred of communism was so great that it led him to change parties for the second time in his career.

There was now a new political party in Britain: the Labour Party. It was a socialist party, not a communist one, but Churchill thought it might become a communist party one day. He believed that if the Labour Party were elected to government, it would be a national disaster.

Churchill had always been independent and

unwilling to toe his own party's line on every single issue. He had had quarrels with his party in the days when he was a Conservative, and he had had quarrels with his party since becoming a Liberal.

However, after a general election in December 1923, the Liberal Party did something Churchill thought unforgiveable. They made a deal with the Labour Party which helped Labour to form its first ever government.

And so Churchill left the Liberal Party. When, just a year later, there was another general election, Churchill won a seat and became an MP again. But now, after twenty years, he had come back to his old party: he was a Conservative once more.

Not all Conservatives, though, were happy to welcome him back.

# 11

# The Rise of Hitler

Churchill was wrong about a Labour government being a national disaster. He also soon saw he had been wrong to worry about Germany becoming a communist state. Instead, something else was happening in Germany – and it was something that alarmed Churchill just as much.

After the First World War a new political party had emerged in Germany called the Nazi Party. Its leader was Adolf Hitler. At first the Nazis took part in elections, but once Hitler was appointed German Chancellor (the head of the government) he had laws passed which gave him total power.

Churchill was one of several British MPs who were very worried about this. Many times, he raised his concerns in the House of Commons. "We were told after the Great War that Germany would be a democracy with a Parliament," he said to his fellow MPs. "For a while, it was. But now all that has been swept away. You have a dictatorship – a most grim dictatorship. You have militarism and appeals to every form of fighting spirit, as well as this persecution of the Jews, which appals everyone who feels that men and women have a right to live in the world where they are born, and have a right to pursue a livelihood, too."

Hitler and the Nazi Party were saying that Germany had lost the First World War because its war effort had been sabotaged by 'non-German' groups inside Germany. The main group it blamed was the Jews, despite the fact that thousands of German Jewish soldiers had fought and died in the war.

Now, on the order of the Nazis, Jewish shops were boycotted, Jews were thrown out of their jobs, and armed thugs who attacked Jews, instead of being punished, were hailed as heroes.

Racist anti-Jewish feeling was common in Europe at that time, but Churchill had always passionately disagreed with it. Now, seeing the Nazi Party making brutal anti-Jewish racism part of official government policy, Churchill was horrified.

Another of the Nazis' frightening policies involved territorial expansion. The Nazis believed that the Germans were a master race, and should inhabit a great empire. They needed more room – more land – to live in. They wanted to invade and occupy other countries.

And so they began, secretly at first, to rearm for war.

The treaties made at the end of the First World War had included strict rules to make sure German military strength was kept below that of the Allies (the countries who had fought against Germany). Now news began to leak out of Germany that it was breaking the treaties. It was building up its army and navy, and building a powerful air force, the Luftwaffe. Churchill was especially worried about the air force, because it could be built up more quickly than the other armed forces, and was a new and terrifying form of military strength against which no country yet had proper defences.

Time and again, Churchill spoke in Parliament about the danger of German rearmament. He argued that Britain must build up her own military strength – especially her air force – to keep pace with Germany. Some civil servants working for government departments agreed with him, and secretly passed him information, to help him argue his case in Parliament.

But the government did not listen. Ever since the end of the First World War, there had been a strong popular peace movement in Britain. Many politicians argued that European countries should be getting rid of their weapons, not building new ones.

In the summer of 1935, Stanley Baldwin took over as Prime Minister. He was a Conservative – like Churchill – but to Churchill's bitter disappointment, Baldwin did not offer him a government job. Churchill was 60 now. Many people thought he would never hold high office again.

However, despite this disappointment, and despite growing despair at not being listened to, Churchill continued to argue his case in the House of Commons. He told MPs that the Luftwaffe was already as strong as the Royal Air Force – and that this was a disaster for Britain. If Hitler now simply kept his factories and his pilot training schools running, he would automatically not only become stronger than Britain in the air, but would widen the margin, month after month. Hitler, Churchill knew, saw Britain as frightened, weak and incapable of making war.

In July 1935 Churchill's fellow Conservative, Sir Samuel Hoare, made a speech in the Commons answering some of these concerns. He had become Foreign Secretary just one month before, yet he was full of confidence – and disdain. "May I tell the House a story?" he said. "Only yesterday I heard of a small child, a child of one of my friends, who was found surrounded by balloons. When asked why he had so many, the child answered, "I like to make myself afraid by popping." That may be a harmless habit in the case of a child, but it is a dangerous habit in the case of the many alarm-mongers and scaremongers who now seem to take this delight in creating crises, and, if there be crises, in making the crises worse than they would otherwise be."

Conservative backbenchers grinned and nudged each other. They all knew who Sir Samuel was talking about.

"The trouble is," one of them whispered to his neighbour, "Winston *wants* a war. It's the only thing he enjoys."

# 12

# The Rhineland

It was not true that Churchill wanted war. He had seen too many of its horrors with his own eyes. Churchill thought having a strong military force was the best way to avoid war. He knew that Hitler would be unstoppable if he felt confident that no other country was strong enough to beat him.

The treaties made at the end of the First World War had made a strip of land along Germany's border with the Netherlands, Belgium and France – called 'the Rhineland' – into a 'demilitarised zone'. This meant that Germany was not allowed to move troops into this area, build defences or take part in any other military activity there. It was intended to be a safe buffer zone between old enemies.

On March 7th 1936, Hitler stood up in the German Parliament and announced his intention to reoccupy the Rhineland. Even as he spoke, German troops flooded into the area.

Europe was horrified. Five days later the French Foreign Minister, Monsieur Flandin, came to see Churchill at his London flat. With Flandin came Ralph Wigram, one of the civil servants who had passed information to Churchill.

Churchill welcomed them both into his drawing room and asked Flandin whether he had yet spoken to any government ministers.

Flandin nodded. "The Prime Minister, the Foreign Secretary and the Chancellor of the Exchequer," he said, accepting Churchill's offer of a seat. "I proposed to them that, in response to Germany's violation of the treaties, Britain and France together should mobilise our land, sea and air forces. Czechoslovakia, Romania and Yugoslavia have already sent messages to say they will support us."

"Good, good," said Churchill, pacing in front of the fireplace. "I have no doubt whatsoever that we have superior strength. We only have to act, and Hitler will be forced to withdraw. What was the response?"

Flandin ran a hand anxiously through his hair. "The Prime Minister said he did not know a great deal about foreign affairs, but he did know the feelings of the British people. And he said they want peace."

"If only he knew how to get it for them!" muttered Churchill.

"He also said," Flandin went on, "that if there is even one chance in a hundred that war would be the result of acting over the Rhineland, then he could not commit Britain to do it. He said Britain is not ready to go to war."

"Ha! And whose fault is that?" Churchill said. He offered Flandin a cigar, then took one for himself. "If I were in the government you would have received a different answer. But France is strong enough to act alone. With Hitler's army at its present size, France can push the Germans back, even if Britain will not help. Next year, that may not still be so. You must act, sir!"

Flandin groaned. "French opinion is divided. The people fear another war as much as the British do. I do not believe that France can mobilise unless she is backed by the will of Britain."

When Flandin had left, Churchill carried on pacing the room. Wigram sank heavily into a chair.

"War is inevitable, now, isn't it?" Wigram said, covering his face with his hands. "And it will be the most terrible war there has ever been."

# 13

# The Munich Agreement

In marching his troops into the Rhineland in 1936, Hitler took a huge gamble. His army was not yet strong enough to fight France, let alone France and Britain together. But, to the astonishment of Hitler's generals – some of whom had hoped the Rhineland would be Hitler's downfall – the gamble paid off. France did nothing. Britain did nothing.

For the next two years, Hitler set about increasing his military strength. A vast 'West Wall' of fortifications was built in the Rhineland. His armed forces grew larger. His munitions factories poured out weapons and war supplies. By 1938, Hitler knew he wouldn't have to take any more gambles. Germany was now strong enough to dominate Europe.

For many years, Hitler had made it clear that he

thought Austria and Germany should be united as one country. On March 12th 1938, German troops occupied Austria. The Austrian Nazi Party had been undermining the government there for years, the Austrian Chancellor had already been assassinated, and when the German troops moved in, they were almost unopposed. Hitler declared that Austria was now part of Germany.

With Austria in German hands, Czechoslovakia was almost completely surrounded by German territory. It seemed obvious that Hitler would want to invade Czechoslovakia next.

In Britain, a Conservative named Neville Chamberlain had taken over from Stanley Baldwin as Prime Minister. Churchill urged Chamberlain that the best way to combat Hitler was to make an alliance between Britain, France and the Soviet Union. "You know how strongly I am opposed to communism," he told Chamberlain. "I hope you will appreciate, therefore, that I would not say this unless it were absolutely vital. But vital it most certainly is!"

Chamberlain, however, felt an alliance with the Soviet Union would never work. And he believed neither Britain nor France could possibly save Czechoslovakia from Hitler.

In western Czechoslovakia there was an area called the Sudetenland. The people who lived there were mostly of German origin. Hitler now demanded the Sudetenland for Germany.

Throughout September 1938, Churchill went to see the Prime Minister and the Foreign Secretary again and again. "Tell Germany," he urged them, "that if she sets foot in Czechoslovakia we shall be at war with her immediately."

But Chamberlain was convinced that, if Europe made a deal with Hitler over the Sudetenland, he would not invade the rest of Czechoslovakia.

Three times Chamberlain flew to Germany for meetings with Hitler. The last meeting was held in Munich. The leaders of France and Italy attended too, but the Soviet Union was not invited and nor were the Czechs themselves.

While Chamberlain was away in Munich, Churchill attended a meeting of 'The Other Club' – a dining club for politicians, which he had set up himself before the First World War. He was agitated and angry.

"To win we must act!" he declared, banging the table so hard that the cutlery rattled. "We cannot stand still and allow ourselves to be hit and hit and hit again!"

Two government ministers were present at the dinner. Churchill fixed them with a scorching look. "How can honourable men go along with such a cowardly policy?" he roared.

Before the end of the evening the government ministers made their excuses and slunk away. Churchill and a few others stayed late at the table – so late that one of them went out to buy early editions of the next morning's newspapers. Churchill and his friends sat reading them, and were appalled by the news from Munich. Chamberlain had given in completely to Hitler's demands.

Grief-stricken and fearful for the future, Churchill left the room and made his way out of the hotel where the dinner had been held. He passed an open door; beyond it he saw a party in full swing. "Those poor people," Churchill muttered to himself, watching the people dancing and laughing. "They have no idea what they will have to face."

* * *

Chamberlain flew back to England from his meeting with Hitler and was greeted by jubilant crowds, who were overjoyed that he had saved the country from war. He waved the agreement that he and Hitler had signed. "This is peace with honour!" he announced. "Peace for our time!"

In the Commons, MPs held a debate on the Munich agreement. Many of them congratulated Chamberlain. Then Churchill rose to speak. "I will begin by saying the most unpopular and most unwelcome thing," he said. "I will begin by saying what everybody would like to ignore or forget but which must nevertheless be stated, namely, that we have sustained a total defeat."

At this, other MPs made so much noise – shouting "Nonsense!" and "Ridiculous!" – that Churchill had to pause.

At last he went on: "All is over. Silent, mournful, abandoned, broken, Czechoslovakia recedes into the darkness... It is a tragedy which has occurred.

"I venture to think that in future the

Czechoslovak State cannot be maintained as an independent entity. You will find that in a period of time which may be measured by years, but may be measured only by months, Czechoslovakia will be engulfed in the Nazi regime."

The next speaker referred to Churchill's fears as hysterical. But they were proved right. Five months later, the rest of Czechoslovakia was taken over by the Nazis.

# 14

# Back to the War Cabinet

"Have you seen the poster in the Strand?"

Neville Chamberlain looked up from his desk. "*Another* one?"

His Private Secretary nodded. "It's enormous. 'WHAT PRICE CHURCHILL?' it says, in letters as high as a double-decker bus." He put a file of papers on the Prime Minister's desk. "Our man in Berlin says Churchill is the only Englishman Hitler is afraid of," he added. "He advised giving him a government post."

Chamberlain sighed wearily. "I do not think I could bear it. Discussing an issue with Winston is like arguing with a brass band." He opened the file and scanned the first document. "Besides, I do not believe that Herr Hitler really wants war. But if Winston got into government... by golly, war is what we would all get!"

Not far away, in his flat in Morpeth Terrace, Churchill was at his desk too. Clementine entered the room.

"Winston," she said, "I've just heard on the wireless that Russia has signed an agreement with Germany. Can this be true?"

"I'm afraid so, my darling," Churchill replied. "I cannot believe what this government has thrown away. Russia *offered us an alliance!*"

"Then how can Russia have had such a change of heart?"

Churchill took off his spectacles and turned to face his wife. "Britain, I am afraid, ignored the offer. Now of course the Nazis do not need to worry about their eastern frontier. They can concentrate all resources on their next conquest – which is bound to be Poland. Poor Poland! We must fight for her. We will."

Even Chamberlain now saw that Hitler would stop at nothing. Recognising the threat Germany posed to Poland, the British and Polish governments signed a formal Treaty of Alliance on August 25th 1939. Less than a week later, Hitler's armies invaded Poland. Fulfilling the terms of the treaty, Britain declared war.

Chamberlain summoned Churchill to see him at Downing Street.

"I would like to offer you a place in the War Cabinet," said Chamberlain. *What will Winston say?* he wondered. *Will he crow? Will he ask me to admit he has been right all along?*

But Churchill simply bowed his head respectfully and said, "I accept. Thank you, Prime Minister."

The job Chamberlain gave Churchill was First Lord of the Admiralty – the same job he had held at the outbreak of the First World War. A signal was flashed to the ships of the fleet: "Winston is back!"

That same afternoon Churchill strode into the First Lord's room at the Admiralty, with one of his secretaries, Miss Hill, hurrying behind him. He walked up to the wooden panelling and flung open the concealed doors of a wall-cupboard. Revealed was a large map, dotted with coloured pins representing British and German ships... from the last war.

"Ah good – it's still here!" exclaimed Churchill, rubbing his hands. "I shall be needing this!"

# 15
# Preparing for War

"Take this down, Miss Hill." Churchill was standing at his desk, leafing through documents. "All merchant ships must be armed as quickly as possible. All naval vessels must be fitted with Range and Direction Finding equipment." ('Range and Direction Finding' was a new detection system that would later be called Radar.)

He paused, and read for a moment. Then he said, "I want a report on the progress of the 'sticky bomb' idea. Shut that window, would you? There's a cold draught."

As Miss Hill hurried to the window, he added, "That reminds me: the sailors on our destroyers. Have enough warm duffle coats been issued for them for the winter?"

On Churchill's desk here in the First Lord's room,

beside heaps of documents and reports – topped with military medals used as paperweights – lay a pile of bright red labels bearing the words 'Action This Day'. Churchill attached them to every urgent order. Of which there were many.

With Churchill in the building, the Admiralty buzzed – with energy, with determination, with *fight*. The staff were exhausted, exasperated and inspired.

"Will that be all, sir?"

Churchill blinked at Miss Hill, thinking for a moment about submarine deployment. It was three o'clock in the morning. He glanced at the clock and noticed, for once, how tired his secretary looked. "Yes, I suppose so. And Miss Hill..." he added, as she got up to go.

"Yes, Mr. Churchill?"

"No need to rush in in the morning." He waved a hand as he went back to his work. "Eight o'clock will be fine."

# 16
# Prime Minister

By May 1940, seven months after declaring war on Germany, the British government was in crisis. The newspapers, the public and the House of Commons had lost faith in Neville Chamberlain's leadership. There were calls for his resignation.

At 11 o'clock on May 10th, Churchill was summoned to see Chamberlain at Downing Street. Another member of the War Cabinet, Lord Halifax, was summoned too.

Chamberlain was waiting for them in the Cabinet Room. "Gentlemen," he said, "a Conservative government alone cannot carry the burden of leading the country through this war. We need a government uniting all the parties. But the Labour Party refuses to serve under my leadership. There will have to be a new Prime Minister."

Chamberlain coolly surveyed the two men he had summoned: tall, gaunt Halifax and Churchill – stocky, solid and bristling with energy. Chamberlain wanted Halifax to succeed him. Halifax was the King's choice too. But many people, he knew, were calling for Churchill. Now he hoped Churchill would say, voluntarily, that he would be happy to serve under Halifax.

There was a long silence. Churchill – who usually spoke more than anyone else at meetings – had never been so quiet.

At last it was Lord Halifax who spoke. "I do not believe that I – sitting in the House of Lords rather than the House of Commons, as I do – could be an effective leader of the government. Were His Majesty to ask me to form a government, I am afraid I should refuse."

Chamberlain thanked them both and the meeting ended. Churchill returned to the Admiralty, where vast amounts of work awaited him. The previous night, huge forces of German troops had surged across the borders of Holland, Belgium and Luxembourg. Telegrams were pouring in, updating Churchill with news of the fighting. Thoughts of the leadership were pushed to the back of his mind.

Then, at six o'clock, Churchill was summoned to Buckingham Palace. Chamberlain had visited the King and resigned. He had recommended that the King should ask Churchill to form a government – which he did.

And so, at 65 years of age, Winston Churchill became Prime Minister.

That night, Churchill stayed up working until 3 a.m. When at last he collapsed into bed he felt a huge sense of relief. At last *he* could make the decisions. At last *he* could direct the war. He felt as though the whole 65 years of his life so far had been a preparation for this task. It had been his destiny.

"I have nothing to offer but blood, toil, tears and sweat," he told the Commons three days later. His voice boomed – resolute, sombre and strong. "We have before us an ordeal of the most grievous kind. We have before us many, many long months of struggle and of suffering.

"You ask, what is our policy? I will say: It is to wage war, by sea, land and air, with all our might

71

and with all the strength that God can give us; to wage war against a monstrous tyranny never surpassed in the dark, lamentable catalogue of human crime. That is our policy.

"You ask, what is our aim? I can answer in one word: It is victory, victory at all costs, victory in spite of all terror, victory, however long and hard the road may be; for without victory, there is no survival."

# 17
# A Dark Day for France

"Mr Churchill, sir?"

Under the bedclothes Churchill stirred and blearily opened his eyes. "Yes, what is it?"

"I'm sorry to wake you, sir, but the Prime Minister of France is on the telephone for you. This line here." The man indicated Churchill's bedside table.

Instantly, Churchill was fully alert. He leaned up on his elbow and picked up the receiver. "Monsieur Reynaud?"

The voice of Reynaud, Prime Minister of France, came down the line: "We have been defeated."

*It has happened*, thought Churchill. The Germans have invaded France.

This was only his fifth day as Prime Minister.

He said, "The great French army? Beaten in the

course of one night? Surely that is not possible?"

Reynaud's voice sounded anguished. "The German troops have crossed right through Belgium and broken our front line near the town of Sedan. They have tanks and armoured cars. Their speed is astonishing."

Churchill sat up in bed. "If they have broken through the front line they cannot advance indefinitely. They will have to halt for supplies. We must plan a counter-attack."

But Reynaud only said again, "We are defeated. We have lost the battle."

With the telephone still pressed to his ear, Churchill threw back the blankets and swung his legs out of bed. "I will be in Paris as soon as I can. Have courage, sir. We will beat them yet."

\* \* \*

The small plane landed at Le Bourget airport.

As French army officers walked forward to greet Churchill, he asked them, "What is the latest news?"

"The Germans are expected to reach Paris in a matter of days, sir."

Churchill's expression darkened. "Then it is worse than I thought."

He was taken to the Ministry of Foreign Affairs in Paris – a huge and sumptuous building, decorated like a royal palace. There he met Prime Minister Reynaud, as well as the French Minister of National Defence and War, and General Gamelin, the French Commander-in-Chief. All three looked downcast.

"The situation is grave, gentlemen," said Churchill, "but it is far from hopeless. Together we must plan our counter-attack. Firstly and most importantly – where is your strategic reserve?"

The strategic reserve is the section of an army that is kept back from the fighting at the beginning of a battle, so that later it can be sent wherever there is a sudden need. Having a strategic reserve has been part of battle tactics for thousands of years.

General Gamelin shook his head. "We have no reserve."

Churchill was staggered. For a moment he could not say a word. Movement outside the tall windows caught his eye. Elderly men, too old for army service, were walking past, pushing wheelbarrows piled high with files and papers. Some distance away clouds of grey smoke billowed from several large bonfires.

The French government's documents were being burnt. This, Churchill knew, meant the government was preparing to flee Paris. They were certain of defeat.

With an effort, he pulled himself together. "Look. Divisions of troops can be moved from quiet parts of the front. Do you have more divisions abroad? In Africa? Good. They must be brought back immediately. We can attack this corridor of the German advance on both flanks."

Reynaud spoke. "Please – we need you to send us aircraft squadrons. Bombers and fighters. This is the only thing that can save us. Send us all you have."

Churchill nodded. "Certainly we will send you aircraft, as many as we can. I will discuss it with my War Cabinet in London. Believe me, we will do *everything* in our power. But you must stiffen your resolve."

On the flight home Churchill sat beside his Chief Staff Officer, General Ismay.

"It is a dark day for the great French nation," he said. "Her leaders are crumpling."

"If France falls," said Ismay, "who stands with us against the Nazis?"

Churchill looked out of the window, frowning ferociously at the clouds. "No one," he said. "We stand alone."

# 18

# The Fight for Dunkirk

As soon as Britain had declared war on Germany in September 1939, the government had sent ten British army divisions to France. They were known collectively as the British Expeditionary Force, or B.E.F. Now they were struggling alongside their French comrades against the German onslaught.

Soon the German advance had cut right across France to the coast. The B.E.F. and many other Allied troops were trapped north of this German line. They were in dire peril – the Germans were trying to encircle them and cut off any chance of escape by sea.

So the War Cabinet in London commanded the B.E.F. to retreat as fast as possible to the coast. If the troops could reach the sea before the Germans cut them off, they could be evacuated across the Channel.

This was a terrible decision for the War Cabinet to have to make, not only because retreat felt like defeat, but also because, even if the troops could be rescued – which was not at all certain, as the Germans were advancing rapidly – their precious artillery, vehicles and equipment could not. Everything would have to be abandoned, and it would take British factories many months to manufacture replacements.

"But what does the equipment matter, compared to these soldiers?" said Churchill, stalking round the Map Room at Downing Street, smoking a cigar. "They are the heart of the greater army we will build for next year and the years beyond that." He stopped and turned to one of his military advisers. "How many troops can we evacuate?"

"They will have to be brought off the beaches under attack from the Luftwaffe," said the adviser.

"How many?" repeated Churchill.

"Forty-five thousand over two days. Perhaps fifty thousand, maximum."

Churchill chewed on his cigar. He knew that the total number of British and Allied troops trapped north of the German line ran into hundreds of thousands.

"We will need small vessels as well as the Royal Navy's ships," he said. "The small ones will be able to push further forward into shallow waters – the men will be able to wade to them. Put out an appeal: say it is for a special requirement – don't give details yet. Anything can be of use: fishing-boats, yachts, pleasure-boats, barges, lifeboats from larger ships – they must all come down to the Channel ports."

"Yes, sir."

As the days of preparation passed, Churchill felt sometimes confident, sometimes desperate. But he never lost his fierce determination to carry on.

"With the Army brought home from France," he told the War Cabinet, "I believe we will be able to hold out here." Others in his War Cabinet, however, did not share his certainty.

It was late May. In the garden of No. 10 Downing Street the trees were in full blossom. Bees hummed over the flowers. The sky was clear – it was a day of breathtaking beauty.

Churchill and Lord Halifax were walking together on the lawn. Recent meetings of the War

Cabinet had been very tense. Now, despite the glorious weather, their conversation was fraught.

"I am no coward, Winston," said Halifax. "You think I am a pessimist. I believe I am a realist. We must find some way to make peace with Hitler. Accept that he will dominate Europe, but save Britain's independence. I cannot bear the thought that this country will be crushed along with so many others."

Churchill took his cigar from his mouth. "I respect your view and the patriotic sentiments that lie behind it," he said, as steadily as he could. "But I must urge you to consider the reality of making terms with such a barbarous regime. Hitler would not respect an independent Britain. We would become a slave state." He stopped and looked up at a nearby tree. A bird, right at the top, was singing its heart out. He said, "It is better to go down fighting. To go down in a blaze of glory that does honour to the history of our great nation."

Churchill turned to Halifax. "My lord, if you resign over this, the government will collapse. The trust that the British people have invested in us will be squandered. Their brave resolve will be

81

shattered – irreparably. I beg you to hold firm. I beg you to trust that we can win."

Over the space of three days, nine meetings of the War Cabinet were held. Churchill's position as Prime Minister – less than a month old – hung in the balance. At the end of those three days, to Churchill's intense relief, Halifax did hold firm. He accepted that there would be no negotiations with Hitler, and he did not resign.

Meanwhile the French port of Dunkirk was chosen as the place the retreating troops should fight their way back to, and from which as many of them as possible would be rescued and brought to England.

The fighting was ferocious; the Germans were determined to cut off the route to Dunkirk. In an attempt to stop them, a small force of British soldiers was fighting desperately at Calais, further down the coast, holding up the German advance for as long as they could.

Churchill and his commanders now took a heart-wrenching decision.

"Every hour the Calais troops continue to fight is invaluable," said Churchill. "I must send a telegram, and tell them they will not be evacuated. We need all the time they can give us to get the bulk of the army to Dunkirk. They must fight to the death."

That evening Churchill had dinner at Admiralty House with the Secretary of State for War, Anthony Eden, and the Commander-in-Chief of the British Army, General Ironside. Usually, dinners with Churchill were lively and entertaining – but tonight he was quiet.

"Are you quite well, Winston?" asked Eden.

Churchill pushed his plate away and rested his forehead on his hands. Without moving, he said, "We have so few trained troops. To sacrifice such splendid, brave men at Calais... it makes me feel sick. I cannot eat." His deep, rumbling voice sounded grief-stricken. "God knows I hope their sacrifice will not be in vain. We have done all we can for Dunkirk. But will it be enough?"

# 19
# The Mosquito Armada

The response to Churchill's appeal for small vessels to help in the evacuation of Dunkirk was overwhelming. Hundreds of small boats – called 'the Mosquito Armada' – set out for the French coast.

At the beaches around Dunkirk, soldiers sheltered among the sand dunes from the Luftwaffe bombardment, or stood up to their shoulders in water, some for hours at a time, waiting to be picked up. The Luftwaffe had been ordered to destroy the retreating army and the ships that came to save them. This would be a huge victory for the Nazis, crushing Britain's ability to carry on fighting.

For more than a week the boats plied back and forth between France and England, at first in daylight and then, when the losses from German bombs, torpedoes and mines became too heavy, only at night. When the operation's commanders thought they were finished, Churchill sent them back again, to make sure that they had picked up not just the British, but as many French and other Allied troops as they possibly could.

Meanwhile, up in the skies, the Royal Air Force – despite being outnumbered by the Luftwaffe – beat the Germans back. The evacuation was a triumphant success. Churchill had thought no more than 50,000 troops could be rescued. In fact more than 338,000 men escaped, including almost 140,000 French, Polish, Dutch and Belgian soldiers.

While the operation was in progress, somehow Churchill found time for the painstaking and laborious process of writing one of his most inspiring speeches. He delivered it in the House of Commons – and repeated it over the radio so that the whole nation could hear it – just hours after the last soldiers had been brought back from Dunkirk.

"Even though large tracts of Europe and many old and famous States have fallen or may fall into the grip of the Gestapo and all the odious apparatus of Nazi rule," he said, "we shall not flag or fail. We shall go on to the end."

In Parliament many Conservative MPs, bearing old grudges, listened coldly, still not wholeheartedly supporting his leadership. On the Labour benches, however, several MPs were moved to tears as he went on:

"We shall fight in France, we shall fight on the seas and oceans, we shall fight with growing confidence and growing strength in the air; we shall defend our Island, whatever the cost may be.

"We shall fight on the beaches, we shall fight on the landing-grounds, we shall fight in the fields and in the streets, we shall fight in the hills. We shall never surrender.

"And even if, which I do not for a moment believe, this Island or a large part of it were subjugated and starving, then our Empire beyond the seas, armed and guarded by the British Fleet, would carry on the struggle, until, in God's good time, the New World, with all its power and might, steps forth to the rescue and liberation of the Old."

# 20

# Home Guard

When he talked about the 'New World' coming to the rescue of the Old, the main country Churchill was thinking of was the United States of America. He believed that one day, America would join with Britain to defeat Germany. How and when this would happen, he did not know.

The American President, Franklin D. Roosevelt, was sympathetic to Britain's situation, but he was firmly resolved to keep America out of the war. What's more, many of his advisers were convinced that Britain was already beaten and that her surrender to Germany was inevitable.

Britain was certainly vulnerable. Though the rescue of the troops from Dunkirk had been triumphantly accomplished against the odds, what had happened was still a military disaster.

Having abandoned thousands of guns and vehicles and almost seven hundred tanks in France, the British Army only had enough equipment for two divisions of troops. Churchill now dispatched these two divisions straight back to France to help resist the ever-deadlier German advance.

This meant that Britain was left almost entirely disarmed, and with all the Channel ports in France, Belgium and the Netherlands now in Nazi hands, the country needed to make use of every defensive measure it could. What meticulously worked-out plan, Churchill wondered, was next on Hitler's list? What new weapons was he developing? Which coast of Britain would he attack first?

Churchill planned in detail how the population could best fight the Nazis if they did invade. Nine months before, while still at the Admiralty, he had called for a 'Home Guard' to be formed, recruiting men who were too old to join the regular forces but wanted to defend their country. Now it was done, and the response from the public was enormous. There were no uniforms at first, and no weapons, but sporting rifles, farmers' and gamekeepers' guns and homemade clubs and spears were kept ready in the meantime. Churchill practised with his own gun at a shooting range, so he'd be ready for the fight himself. However poorly equipped Britain was, he was confident every inch of ground would be fiercely defended, even to the death. And he had come up with a slogan to use if the invasion happened:

'YOU CAN ALWAYS TAKE ONE WITH YOU.'

# 21
# The Battle of Britain

"Gentlemen, France has surrendered." Churchill leant forward, looking up and down the table at his Cabinet colleagues. "And she has done it without honouring a vital pledge she made to us: that on no account, whatever happened, would the French fleet fall into German hands." He glowered, as if the people before him were responsible. "The French admirals needed only to command their ships to sail to British or neutral ports. But this they have not done.

"As a result, world naval power hangs in the balance. If the French fleet is added to the German fleet, the Nazis will have mastery of the seas. Our supplies will be cut off – we will not survive. At all costs, this cannot be allowed to happen. I propose, gentlemen, heart-breaking though it is to act against sailors who were our allies just days ago, that if the French ships, wherever they are in the world, cannot be brought under British control they must be sunk."

"I agree wholeheartedly," said Anthony Eden, the Secretary of State for War. "There is no other option."

This ruthless decision took huge courage at a moment when Britain was entirely alone. And though many of the French ships co-operated with Britain, some did not. At Oran in Algeria the British Navy and Air Force killed more than one thousand French sailors.

Churchill was fully expecting to be condemned for this. Instead, to his surprise, the whole of the House of Commons recognised how vital this awful move had been and cheered Churchill to the rafters – even the Conservative MPs who had mistrusted him for so long. In America, the attack on the French fleet made government officials realise that Churchill's speeches about fighting to the end were not just brave words: he meant it. There was no more talk of Britain being already beaten.

However, a determination to fight to the end still did not guarantee that victory was possible. President Roosevelt had authorised the sending of American rifles and ammunition to the British Army – a decision Churchill hugely appreciated – but Britain was still in a dreadful position: it would be months before the weapons and vehicles lost at Dunkirk could be replaced.

What's more, Churchill now knew for certain, from German messages intercepted by British intelligence services, that Hitler was planning the invasion of Britain, codenamed 'Operation Sea Lion'.

"Our fate depends on victory in the air," he told his Cabinet. "By destroying the French fleet we have denied Hitler naval supremacy. Without naval supremacy, he cannot invade unless he has air supremacy. He will not be able to bring his army across the Channel under bombardment from our air force. I predict that his plan, therefore, will be for the Luftwaffe to destroy the RAF and our airfields between London and the south coast of England. This will be the battle on which our future depends."

It was just as Churchill predicted. To prepare the way for a Nazi invasion of Britain, the Luftwaffe attacked, aiming to destroy the RAF and its airfields. The resulting 'Battle of Britain' was to last four months – four months of intense anxiety for Churchill.

Churchill's enthusiasm for aeroplanes had never waned, and now he took a great interest in the air battles. Several times when staying at Chequers – the Prime Minister's country home – he visited the headquarters of No. 11 Fighter Group at Uxbridge, in the hope of seeing the command of an air battle from the underground Operations Room there. One such visit occurred on Sunday September 15th, 1940.

As Churchill and Clementine climbed out of their chauffeur-driven car, they were met by Air Vice-Marshal Keith Park, a New Zealander who had been a flying ace in the First World War, and was now – as commander of No.11 Fighter Group – responsible for the air defence of south-east England.

Churchill said, "The weather is fine today. Do you think the Luftwaffe will take advantage?"

"All's quiet at the moment, sir," replied Park, leading his guests down the long staircase into the bomb-proof bunker, sixty feet below ground.

Their destination was the Operations Room, where a huge map of the Channel and the English and French coastlines was laid out on a vast table. Dotted about on its surface stood small blocks of wood displaying numbers. Each block represented British or enemy aircraft and, as news of the aircrafts' locations – received from Radar and the Observer Corps – came in, staff moved the blocks about on the map table using special sticks.

On the wall above the table hung a huge board on which coloured lights indicated the status of each squadron. Different colours meant 'At Standby', 'Enemy Sighted', 'In Action', 'Ordered to Land'. Weather conditions were also shown, using coloured discs.

Soon, as Churchill and Clementine watched, the staff at the table started to move about, pushing markers into position. A Luftwaffe attacking force had set off from France. The lights on the board began to glow as squadrons were put on standby and then took off to enter battle.

Churchill sat fascinated as Air Vice-Marshal Park walked up and down, watching the battle, supervising his staff, and calmly giving orders – deciding how many fighter squadrons to scramble, and when and how to use them.

At last Churchill looked up at the board and saw that all the lights were red. All the squadrons were in action at once.

"What reserves do we have?" he asked.

"I have telephoned No. 12 Group," Park replied, "to ask for three more squadrons to cover London and our fighter airfields. They are now in action too."

"And beyond that?"

"None, sir."

If more waves of Luftwaffe planes came over now, the RAF would have nothing with which to meet them. The atmosphere in the Operations Room was tense. Everyone knew what was at stake.

But more planes did not come. And, at last, the movement of the markers on the map table showed that the Luftwaffe were heading eastwards again, back to their bases.

"We are very glad, sir, that you have seen this,"

said Air Vice-Marshal Park as he accompanied Churchill and Clementine back to their car. "The Air Force was strained to the limit today. It is good that you understand the gravity of our situation at times like this."

"I am glad that I have seen it too," said Churchill. "The devotion of your team, and the courage and skill of the pilots you command is turning the tide of world war."

As Churchill had told his fellow MPs in Parliament just three weeks before, paying tribute to the RAF pilots: "Never in the field of human conflict was so much owed by so many to so few."

# 22
# The Blitz

In the autumn of 1940, the Luftwaffe – having failed to destroy the RAF – changed their tactics. They began mass bombings of London and many other British towns and cities. They wanted to destroy factories, shipyards and docks, to cut communications and to terrorise the British people.

Churchill knew that the battle to keep Britain's morale high in the face of such an onslaught was as important as any other kind of battle. He toured the country visiting bomb-damaged areas, never without his trademark cigar, and always with an expression on his face in which sorrow was mixed with stubborn defiance. In September 1940, on a visit to bomb-wrecked area of the East End of London, the people who had gathered to greet Churchill saw his eyes fill with tears.

"Look, he really cares!" shouted a woman in the crowd. All around her, people began cheering.

"We can take it!" a voice cried out.

"Give it 'em back!" yelled another.

Respect for Churchill was hugely increased by the fact that during the German raids, far from fleeing the bombs, he liked to get as close to them as possible. His favourite place from which to watch an attack – to the dismay of his anxious staff – was on the nearest roof or turret-top.

For safety, the Cabinet met at this time in a specially built underground bunker, called the Cabinet War Rooms. It was in fact an entire underground command centre, complete with bedrooms for Churchill, his ministers and his military advisers, BBC broadcasting equipment, a telephone switchboard and a Map Room which was staffed night and day by army, navy and air force officers, who monitored the worldwide military situation and produced daily reports.

But no matter how bad the nightly bombing raids became, Churchill did not like to sleep at the

War Rooms. He preferred to stay above ground. No. 10 Downing Street was considered ill-built and rickety and therefore dangerous to spend the night in, so he often used a flat near the War Rooms called the 'No. 10 Annexe'.

Churchill's favourite safety tactic, though, was to move about frequently. His devoted but exasperated secretaries and assistants rarely knew in advance where he would settle to do his work – during the day or at night – and had always to be ready to scoop up as many vital papers as they could and hurry after him when he set off for a change of venue.

Life in the bombed cities was hard. Night after night hundreds of people were killed, thousands more made homeless. Frightened and weary families crowded together in shelters. Drains were smashed. Electricity and gas supplies were cut off. Fires raged. Yet still the factories had to be kept open – when the people emerged after the 'All Clear' had sounded, they had to do their day's work. No one knew when or how this reign of terror would end. There was no guarantee that it would not simply keep on getting worse.

Nevertheless, Churchill believed Britain was holding up well. His main concern was that Hitler might launch 'Operation Sea Lion' just at this moment when the country was so battered. Churchill knew from Intelligence reports that troops were gathered at the Nazi-occupied Channel Ports, preparing to invade Britain.

On October 27th 1940, a British listening-post picked up a secret German radio message that was being sent to these troops. Like so many other secret messages sent by the Nazis, it had been encrypted using their 'Enigma' machine – a machine that produced a very complicated system of codes. The Nazis believed the Enigma codes were unbreakable. But at Bletchley Park in Buckinghamshire, British mathematicians and code experts had been working relentlessly to decrypt them and had succeeded. The information gained this way had already saved many lives. Now it brought Churchill a piece of momentous news.

The troops must continue their training for Operation Sea Lion according to plan. *Well*, he thought, *if training is still in progress, the invasion can't be about to begin, can it?*

The next day, photographs taken from a British reconnaissance plane showed Nazi ships moving away from Britain. Any doubts remaining in Churchill's mind vanished.

"This is proof positive," he said to the Intelligence officer who had brought him the news. "Hitler has changed his mind. The Nazi invasion is not imminent. And with winter coming on, he will have to delay for several months at the very least. We have won a breathing space!"

# 23

# Pearl Harbour

Though Churchill did not yet know it, Operation Sea Lion had been postponed indefinitely. The following spring, Hitler abandoned his plan to invade Britain in favour of an even bolder plan: to invade the Soviet Union.

Just like the leaders of Germany during the First World War, Hitler hated and feared the Slav peoples of Europe, such as Russians and Poles. His ambition, therefore, had always been to invade the Soviet Union. However, in 1939 it had suited Nazi Germany to sign a pact with the Soviet government, agreeing that they would not attack one another.

Now Hitler was ready to tear up that agreement. Churchill had gleaned from secret German messages decrypted at Bletchley that an attack on the Soviets was likely. When at last news came

– on 22nd June 1941 – that the attack had been launched, he spent the entire day composing a speech to deliver by radio broadcast that evening. It was time well spent. Churchill's broadcasts were listened to throughout the world – even, at great risk, by people huddled around secretly-kept radios in Nazi-occupied countries.

In this broadcast, Churchill did not deny what a fierce opponent of communism he had always been. But, he said, Britain had one task now and one task only: to defeat the Nazis. And anyone who fought against the Nazis was Britain's ally.

Though the Soviet Union was ill-equipped and needed Britain to help by sending her own scarce and precious weapons and raw materials, still Churchill was delighted. He knew that the Soviet Union, once she could fight at full strength, would be an immensely powerful ally. To make victory absolutely certain, however, Churchill wanted one more country to join the war on the Allied side: America.

Throughout 1941, Churchill made a huge effort to build up Britain's friendship with America. In the event, however, it was not this friendship that brought America into the war – it was an attack by Germany's ally, Japan. In December 1941, Japanese aircraft bombed American ships in Pearl Harbour, Hawaii. Though sickened by the deaths of more than two thousand sailors, Churchill greeted the news with joy. "Now we will win!" he told his staff. "There is no doubt about it!"

# 24
# The World at War

The European war had become a world war. The new year, 1942, would see battles fought from the Pacific Ocean to the deserts of North Africa, from Burma in South-East Asia to Rzhev on the north-western frontier of Russia.

Meanwhile, the Nazi regime in its occupied territories had become even more barbarous. Hitler and his generals had decided to kill all the Jews in Europe, and camps had been built in Poland, in which millions of Jews – men and women, children and the elderly – were now being put to death.

Churchill was appalled – he considered this the greatest and most horrible crime ever committed in the whole history of the world. Despite mounting exhaustion and increasing bouts of ill-health he began to travel relentlessly – to America for meetings with President Roosevelt, to Egypt to see the British Army's situation there for himself, and to the Soviet Union to meet his new ally, the Soviet leader Joseph Stalin.

It was not an easy time. The Japanese had won victories in British-controlled Malaya and Hong Kong. The British campaign in the North African desert was not going well. Elsewhere, vital British battleships had been sunk and in June the news arrived that a garrison of 35,000 British troops at Tobruk in Libya had been defeated in a surprise attack by a smaller German force. In the House of Commons a motion was debated "that this House has no confidence in the central direction of the war". This was a direct challenge to Churchill's leadership: governments and soldiers all over the world wondered if he would be forced to step down as Prime Minister.

Criticism of Churchill made during the debate was stinging – but he won the vote. Meanwhile, under pressure as he was at home, abroad – in Moscow – he was under even more.

The Soviet leader, Joseph Stalin, was an intimidating host. Dinners began late at night and would last five hours or more. Churchill, though he liked to work late himself, did well to cope with the strain of these tense, exhausting occasions. He had to be constantly on his toes. He did not trust Stalin. Though the full horrors were not yet known of Stalin's treatment of his own people (he had ordered the killing of hundreds of thousands of Soviets in the 1930s), Churchill did know that Stalin was a brutal tyrant. Still, to defeat Hitler, Churchill and Stalin had to find a way to work together.

"How have you been at war so long and not defeated these German beasts?" Stalin said over dinner one night. "Your soldiers must be puny! Puny and afraid! Perhaps they will lose their fear as soon as they begin to *fight*."

This insult was too much to bear. Britain had endured so much – British soldiers had fought, and died, so bravely. Churchill was furious, but he knew he must not let his anger get the better of him. "Mr Stalin..." he said carefully, "I will pardon that remark only on account of the bravery of the Russian Army."

Stalin was impressed with Churchill's strength of spirit and his forceful personality. His comments became more polite. But still he put pressure on him.

"I cannot understand why," he said, "when my Red Army soldiers are fighting so valiantly in the East, you do not fling the whole strength of *your* army into France to open up a Western Front? This will split the German forces – it is the surest way to victory."

Churchill was coming under pressure from America, too, to launch a big attack in France. But it was a tactic about which he had grave reservations.

"We *will* open up a new front in France," he said to Stalin. "But the timing must be right. The Nazi fighting machine must first be weakened. If we throw our full force into France and it is beaten back into the sea, as it was at Dunkirk, we will have made a dreadful error. Hitler will then have a greater chance of victory – or at the least of delaying our own victory for years to come."

This was the last night of Churchill's visit to Moscow. He managed to get away from the dinner table at half past two in the morning – which left just enough time for a meeting with the British Ambassador, a bath, and an inspection of a Soviet guard of honour before his plane took off at 5.30 a.m. No wonder Churchill was exhausted.

# 25
# The Allies Unite

By 1943, Russian and American pressure for an attack on the Western Front in France became overwhelming. Churchill felt he must give his consent, despite his anxieties. Once he had made this decision, he plunged into planning the operation with every bit as much energy as if his doubts had never existed.

"The day of the attack will be called D-Day," he told a meeting in the Cabinet War Rooms. "The time at which the leading vessels will reach the beaches will be called H-Hour. Once this timing has been agreed – or *timings*, I should say, since many different landing places will be involved – we can work backwards to calculate the necessary timing of every other stage of the operation."

Seated around the table were the British military Chiefs of Staff and the senior American general – a dynamic, energetic soldier named Dwight D. Eisenhower.

"I propose that the Allied forces should approach the French coast by moonlight," Eisenhower said now. "But we must look at the tides. If the assault force lands at high tide it will have to come in so far that it will hit the underwater obstacles the Nazis have built. However, if we come in at low tide the troops will have too far to walk across the beaches. They will be exposed and vulnerable to enemy attack."

"How many days each month will give us the right combination of moonlight and tides?" asked Churchill.

"Only two or three," said Eisenhower. "And that's if the weather is good."

During the First World War Churchill had proposed finding a way for tanks to drive straight onto the shore from specially designed boats. Now at last this idea was put into practice. Tank landing craft were designed, and vast floating harbours were built, which could be taken in pieces to

France and constructed there.

Soon General Eisenhower was appointed Supreme Commander of the Allied Expeditionary Force. He decided that the target date for the beginning of this attack – codenamed 'Operation Overlord' – should be in early June 1944.

The whole of southern England became a vast army camp as British and American soldiers prepared for D-Day. It was planned that in the first two days of the assault, 176,000 troops and 20,000 vehicles would be transported across the Channel – as well as thousands of tonnes of equipment and provisions.

On Monday May 15th 1944, a conference was held in St Paul's School in London. The pupils and teachers had been evacuated to the countryside: the school was now the headquarters of Field Marshal Montgomery – or 'Monty', as he was popularly known – one of the most senior British commanders.

In the school hall sat Churchill, King George VI and the commanders of Operation Overlord. The stage usually used by the headmaster for assemblies was covered by an enormous map of the French coast. It showed the Normandy beaches where the landings would take place, and the countryside beyond, into which the troops would advance. The map was tilted at an angle, so that everyone in the hall could see it, and it was strong enough for the commanders to walk about on as they explained the top secret plan.

"The assault will be conducted in two phases," Monty said, standing on Kent with a long baton in his hands. He tapped the baton on his palm. "One: shortly after midnight on D-Day, there will be a parachute landing of 24,000 Allied troops. Two: at 6.30 a.m., the amphibious landing of Allied infantry and armoured divisions on the coast will begin."

He pointed his baton. "The section of coastline over which the landings will take place is fifty miles long. We have divided it into five sectors, bearing the following names: Utah, Omaha, Gold, Juno and Sword."

Churchill was listening intently. Suddenly he leaned towards his Assistant Private Secretary Jock Colville, who was sitting beside him.

"I'm going to be one of the first there," he whispered. "Don't tell the Admiralty, but I'll be given a lift by HMS Belfast. It's all arranged." He smiled mischievously. "What fun to be there before Monty, eh?"

It was some moments before Colville realised that his mouth was hanging open.

Colville might have been shocked – Eisenhower, when he heard, was appalled. The plan was far too dangerous. Churchill, though, remained determined to go. Finally only a direct appeal from the King made him agree not to put to sea on D-Day.

And so, late on June 5th – the night before the assault – Churchill found himself dining alone with his wife Clementine at the No. 10 Annexe, their flat near the Cabinet War Rooms. Churchill was in a sombre mood. After he had finished eating, he went to the Map Room. For a long time he stood gazing at the map of the Channel coastlines of England and France, studying the clusters of pins which showed the positions of the Allied troops, and those of the Germans – given to him by the codebreakers at Bletchley.

Clementine came up and pressed her fingers on his arm. "Darling," she said, "I feel for you so much tonight. This is such an agonising moment – almost too much to bear."

Still looking at the map, Churchill stroked her

hand in gratitude. Then he turned, and his eyes were full of the heaviness of the responsibilities he bore now, and had borne for so many years. "Do you realise," he said, "that by the time you wake up in the morning, twenty thousand men may have been killed?"

# 26
# D-Day

"I must announce to the House," Churchill told the Commons the next day, "that during the night and the early hours of this morning an immense armada of upwards of 4,000 ships, together with several thousand smaller craft, crossed the Channel.

"Massed airborne landings have been successfully effected behind the enemy lines and landings on the beaches are proceeding at various points.

"Reports are coming in in rapid succession. So far the Commanders report that everything is proceeding according to plan. And what a plan! This vast operation is undoubtedly the most complicated and difficult that has ever occurred. It involves tides, wind, waves, visibility – both from the air and the sea – and the combined employment of land, air and naval forces, working more closely together than ever before."

The Normandy landings on D-Day had gone well, and had taken the Germans by surprise. Though months of fierce fighting followed, with the Nazis putting up stiff resistance right through the autumn and winter of 1944, the liberation of Normandy was the beginning of the liberation of Europe.

However, what had seemed in 1940 a far-off dream – the prospect of victory for the Allies and the defeat of Hitler – brought with it now, for Churchill, new and bitter worries.

"Do you know, Anthony," Churchill said to Anthony Eden – now Foreign Secretary – one Sunday at Chequers, "when we were at the Tehran conference last year, when I sat around that table with Roosevelt and Stalin, I felt – for the first time in my life – what a *small* country Britain is!"

He spread his hands, amazed, as if this seemed a preposterous idea.

"On one side of us there is Russia: a huge bear with its paws reaching out to grasp as much of Europe as it can. On the other side: America. More benign, but equally vast. An..." He hesitated, searching for a word.

"Elephant?" suggested Eden grimly, who had never been such an ardent fan of America as Churchill.

Churchill smiled at Eden with understanding. "All right, an elephant, shall we say? And what are we? A poor little donkey caught in between. But the donkey is the only one who knows the right way home!"

The two men stood in the library at Chequers. It was a grey, squally day and every so often the wind threw a splatter of raindrops against the windowpanes. Churchill sighed heavily. "We all respect the sacrifice and fortitude of Russia's Red Army," he said. "We are all grateful. Nevertheless, I have tried to persuade Roosevelt and Eisenhower that communism is the danger Europe will have to face once Hitler has fallen. I have tried to impress upon them the importance of pushing westwards as fast as we can, of reaching Vienna and Prague before the Soviets do."

"What has been the response?"

Churchill shook his head. "It is no use. They have other priorities." He sank into a nearby chair. He felt so tired these days. Sometimes, after meetings in the underground War Rooms, he had to be carried back to the No. 10 Annexe in a chair.

Neatly and elegantly, Eden sat down too. He said, "Don't they see what is happening in Poland?"

"Exactly!" Churchill burst out. "They should! It was for the sake of Poland's freedom that we entered this war! Stalin promised me there would be free and fair elections once the Russians had liberated Poland. I thought he was a man of his word." He banged his fist on the chair-arm. "Poor Poland has passed from one tyranny to another. And this time there is nothing we can do about it."

Eden knew Churchill was right. Deeply disturbed though he was by events in Poland, he knew Britain could not declare war on the Soviet Union. He said, "Winston, we must make sure France is restored to full strength. She will be our partner in balancing the power of the Soviets."

Churchill passed a hand across his face, desperately weary again. "I fear for the post-war world, Anthony. I fear a third world war."

# 27
# V for Victory

High in their tower the bells of St Paul's Cathedral swung, and the peals rang out across the London rooftops, celebrating the news the country had been waiting for: the war in Europe was over at last.

Men, women and children flooded into the streets in towns and cities, waving Union Jack flags, singing, dancing and celebrating together. On the River Thames in London boats tooted their horns and, in the clear sky above, planes roared in a victory fly-past.

It was May 8th 1945, five years almost to the day since Churchill had become Prime Minister.

Just over a week earlier, Hitler had shot himself dead in Berlin, as Stalin's Red Army overran the city. Now two of Hitler's most senior military commanders had signed an unconditional surrender on behalf of the entire armed forces of Nazi Germany.

Exhausted though he had been in the last months, today Churchill was brimming with energy. He had lunch with the King, delivered his victory speech over the radio at 3 p.m. and then repeated it in the House of Commons half an hour later. From there he led his fellow MPs straight to St Margaret's Church – the church where he and Clementine had been married thirty-seven years before – for a service of thanksgiving. Next he took the members of his War Cabinet and his military Chiefs of Staff to Buckingham Palace to meet the royal family. After that he went to the Ministry of Health building in Whitehall, and emerged onto the balcony to greet the crowd of jubilant people packing the street below.

Looking down at their faces, at their happiness and relief, he felt immensely moved. And he thought of all the other faces that could not be there that day: the faces of the thousands of Britons – the millions worldwide – who had lost their lives in six years of war.

"God bless you all," he said to the crowd. "This is your victory!"

"No!" everyone roared back. "It is yours!"

# 28
# The Bombing of Japan

Victory in Europe did not mean that the war was over. British and Commonwealth armed forces were still fighting in Burma, Singapore and Thailand. It was to be another three months before those troops could celebrate VJ Day – Victory over Japan Day.

The war with Japan was finally brought to an end by the dropping of nuclear bombs on the Japanese cities of Hiroshima and Nagasaki. The nuclear bomb was a new weapon, developed by British and American scientists. Though the bombs were dropped by the Americans, Churchill was consulted before the order was given. The carnage caused by these bombs was horrific, but Churchill believed that even more people would have died if the war had gone on.

Meanwhile, great changes had taken place in

British politics. Churchill's wartime government had been a national government, bringing together members of the Conservative, Liberal and Labour Parties. While the war lasted, party differences had been set aside and everyone had concentrated their efforts on gaining victory. However, as victory in Europe approached, ministers and MPs began to look ahead. A general election was due to be held.

For the past few years, having spent so much time travelling abroad, meeting foreign leaders and inspecting military forces, Churchill had left much of the running of home affairs to other government ministers. He was a national figurehead and in the minds of many people he had risen above party politics.

But Churchill was by instinct a fighter, and now he conducted his election campaign with all the gusto he could muster. Many people found it shocking to turn on the radio and hear the familiar voice of national unity – the voice that had inspired them in the bleakest moments of the war – launching savage attacks on the policies of the Labour Party, when only weeks before he had had Labour ministers in his government.

Churchill's broadcasts were much criticised; the criticism hurt him and made him wonder if he had lost his touch. Nevertheless, as he travelled the country attending election meetings and rallies, crowds lined the roadsides to cheer him. The Conservative Party was convinced that he – and they – would win.

Their confidence turned out to be misplaced. Although Churchill kept his seat in Parliament, the Labour Party won the election by a huge margin: their leader, Clement Attlee, was to be the new Prime Minister.

Weary though he was, Churchill was desperately disappointed. He had not expected – with the harder victory so recently won – to face this defeat. Moreover, he was deeply concerned about the balance of power in post-war Europe, and now he had no power to influence events. It was a heavy blow.

The day after the results were announced, Churchill called a meeting of the Cabinet at noon. It was usual for a defeated Prime Minister to take a few days to wind up government business before handing over to his successor. Churchill, however, wanted to leave office straight away. This was to be his farewell meeting.

The Cabinet Room at No. 10 Downing Street is a grand space. At one end, columns support the high ceiling. At the other, long windows look out across Horse Guards Parade to the Admiralty. Down the centre of the room runs a long polished table surrounded by elegant Victorian chairs, used by generations of ministers. As Churchill presided over his meeting here on July 27th 1945, he maintained a brave and dignified face to his colleagues, but inside he felt wretched.

As the ministers left at the end of the meeting, Churchill called Anthony Eden back. "Thirty years of my life have been passed in this room, Anthony," he said. "And I shall never sit in it again."

# 29
# Churchill's Legacy

Churchill did sit in the Cabinet Room again – and as Prime Minister too. After six years as Leader of the Opposition, he led the Conservative Party to victory in the 1951 general election. At almost 77 years of age, Churchill was Prime Minister once more.

All this time, though he had slowed down, he had never stopped working. Helped by a team of contributors, he had composed a monumental six-volume history of the Second World War, which was near to completion. He had been a prolific author now for half a century, and his literary achievements were formidable. In 1953, in recognition of this, he was awarded the Nobel Prize for Literature, both for his books and for the brilliant eloquence of his speeches.

However, much though Churchill was admired

and respected, many people thought that he was now too old for the demanding job of Prime Minister. A new batch of 'Action This Day' stickers was printed, but they were not used. Churchill had lost his driving energy, although he was still deeply concerned about international affairs, and especially about communism. He knew that the Soviet government was a tyranny and that the people living in its power were not free. He said that an 'iron curtain' had descended across Europe, separating the Russian-controlled communist states from their neighbours.

America and the Soviet Union now both had nuclear bombs. Churchill's last great ambition was to be a peacemaker between the world's great superpowers. But age and illness overtook him.

In November 1954 Churchill celebrated his eightieth birthday. The following spring, he resigned as Prime Minister. The new queen, Elizabeth II, offered to make him a duke but Churchill refused and remained an MP until 1964. The following January, aged 90, he died.

A state funeral had been planned already, under the codename 'Operation Hope-Not'. Churchill's coffin, draped in a Union Jack flag, was taken through London by road and by river. The giant cranes on the quays of the Thames dipped as he passed, in salute. His final journey, to the family churchyard near Blenheim Palace, was made by train. At stations through which the train slowly passed, and in fields and roadsides along the way, thousands of people stood in silence to pay their last respects to one of the greatest – perhaps *the* greatest – leader that Britain had ever had.

# Bibliography

*My Early Life* – Winston S. Churchill (Eland, 2000)

*The World Crisis, 1911-1918* – Winston S. Churchill (Penguin Classics, 2007)

*The Second World War* – Winston S. Churchill (*abridged from the original six volumes by Denis Kelly*, Pimlico, 2002)

*Churchill: A Life* – Martin Gilbert (Pimlico, 2000)

*Churchill* – Roy Jenkins (Pan, 2002)

*The Oxford Dictionary of National Biography: Winston Churchill* by Paul Addison (www.oxforddnb.com/view/article/32413?docPos=3)